Chrissy Corr

The Nutcracker
Coloring Book

written
and designed
by
Ellen Jacob

with drawings
by
Leslie Daley

A Learn-by-Coloring Book

Published by Variety Arts Inc., 305 Riverside Drive, Suite 4A, New York, NY 10025.

Bulk discounts and special editions available for fundraising, promotional, or editorial use; call 1-800-221-2154, 1-212-316-0399. For a catalog of our complete line of products, please send your name and address plus $1.00, indicating your area of interest (dance, gymnastics, skating, or swimming).

ISBN #0-937180-09-2
Printed in U.S.A.

The First Nutcracker

Nearly 100 years ago, on December 17, 1892, the curtain rose on the grand stage of the Maryinsky Theater in St. Petersburg, Russia, for the first performance of <u>The Nutcracker</u>. Tsar Alexander III wanted another triumph from his ballet master Marius Petipa and court composer Peter Ilich Tchaikovsky, the winning team that had already given him <u>Swan Lake</u> and <u>Sleeping Beauty</u>. Petipa proposed a story based on a version of <u>The Nutcracker</u> written by Frenchman Alexandre Dumas. Dumas' tale was taken from an older and more frightening original, <u>The Nutcracker and the Mouse King</u> by E.T.A. Hoffman.

When the famous choreographer fell ill shortly after starting the project, his assistant, Lev Ivanov, took over. The ballet flopped despite Tchaikovsky's magnificent score and a lovely pas de deux for the Sugar Plum Fairy and her Cavalier.

<u>The Nutcracker</u> stayed alive long enough for Nikolay Sergueyev from the same Maryinsky Theater to revive it in 1934 for England's Sadler's Wells Ballet. Americans saw their first <u>Nutcracker</u> in New York six years later, a shortened version by the Ballets Russes de Monte Carlo. It was followed by the first full-length American production by William Christensen's San Francisco Ballet in 1944. Next George Balanchine, who had coached Christensen from memories of performing <u>The Nutcracker</u> as a child in Russia, came out with his own work for the New York City Ballet in 1954. Since then the ballet has become a holiday classic, put on by hundreds of professional companies and thousands of home-town dance schools each year. <u>The Nutcracker</u> is probably the best-loved ballet of all time, for it reveals the mysteries and enchantments of Christmas as seen through the eyes of children, our very best selves.

*I*t is Christmas Eve at the well-to-do home of Judge and Mrs. Stahlbaum. Snow is frosting the window panes, but the house is warm and fragrant with the many preparations for the evening's festivities, and there is much happy bustling about. Nuremberg, where they live, is a town known for its wonderful pastries and mechanical toys. It is the perfect place to be at Christmas.

The Stahlbaum children, Fritz, nine, and Clara, seven, are posted outside the living room door hoping to steal glimpses of the treats in store. Although they cooperate now, in most ways they are complete opposites. Fritz is rosy cheeked, well built, and headstrong. Clara is shy and sensitive, with pale blond shoulder-length hair framing her delicate face.

Forbidden to enter the room until invited, they take turns standing guard by the keyhole most of the afternoon. Fritz grows weary, legs slowly sinking under him, and falls asleep heavily against the door. No one notices that night has fallen too.

*S*uddenly the door is flung open. As they run into the living room Clara and Fritz blink their eyes rapidly at the bright light streaming from the magnificent Christmas tree.

The tree is more than double the height of father Stahlbaum. Candy ornaments and small presents dangle from its branches, and it is lit by hundreds of twinkling candles hidden among the leaves.

Nearby stands a pile of larger gifts, splendidly wrapped and tied with big satin bows. There is a wooden horse for Fritz and an entire regiment of toy soldiers in red uniform mounted on tiny white wooden horses. A large, beautiful doll is waiting for Clara. The children have been told that these presents are from their guardian angel, a reward for being good all year.

The guests begin to arrive, close friends with children, uncles, aunts, and grandparents. Wave after wave of refreshments are served and Judge Stahlbaum directs the company in games and dances. The young ones merrily try to guess what's inside their gift-wrapped boxes, as the carved wooden owl on top of the Stahlbaum's old grandfather clock spreads its wings over the delightful proceedings.

Enter Godfather Drosselmeyer, a prominent doctor who is an old family friend. His odd appearance is exceeded only by the mysterious air that surrounds him.

*T*hin as a reed, Drosselmeyer is nearly six feet tall, with a bad stoop and a black patch over one blind eye. He wears a frizzy white wig which he has fashioned out of glass to hide -- not altogether successfully -- his extreme baldness. But his good eye sparkles and takes in everything around him, revealing a warm and bright curiosity. Godfather Drosselmeyer seems to know a person's secret thoughts just by looking at him.

Not only can this good doctor cure human ills, he can repair anything in the house with magic tools he has made himself. A favorite project is the Stahlbaum's antique grandfather clock, which breaks down regularly. Godfather Drosselmeyer is so knowledgeable about the inner workings of living things, he can create mechanical puppets that move and talk, wooden dogs that bark, and toy soldiers that march.

Everyone expects something special from the doctor, and he does not disappoint. He starts by offering three life-size windup toys for the entertainment of the party: a Columbine, a Harlequin, and a Soldier. To the amazement of young and old, the dolls begin to dance.

The children gather around as Godfather
Drosselmeyer offers Clara a very special gift, a
strange wooden doll called a nutcracker "whose origin, as
ancient as that of the city of Nuremberg," he says enigmatically,
"has been lost in the shadows of time." Clara is immediately
enchanted by the little fellow. He is dressed in a tasteful red
velvet soldier's uniform with real-looking black boots. His head
is much too big for his body, but he has a kind expression in his
large blue eyes and sweet, rosy-lipped smile. His long white
cotton beard is very dignified, she thinks.

*D*octor Drosselmeyer demonstrates how -- by pulling down on his wooden cloak -- the little man's mouth can be opened to display two rows of sharp white teeth and then closed again to crack the nuts between them. Clara sets the Nutcracker to work at once. She is thoughtful enough to pick out only the smallest nuts so that her protege is not obliged to open his mouth too wide, which gives him a ridiculous expression.

Fritz has been standing by jealously with a bowl of the biggest, hardest walnuts he can find, intending to test the strength of the Nutcracker. He snatches the doll from Clara's hands and forces the large nuts into its teeth, breaking off a few pieces and causing the jaw to collapse as he bangs the poor Nutcracker's head on the floor.

Clara's loud cries bring Drosselmeyer to the rescue. The doctor expertly bandages

his tiny patient's broken jaw with a handkerchief while Clara tearfully cradles the wounded Nutcracker, unwilling to leave his side.

*S*ince the hour is late, the guests join in one last dance that includes even the littlest children. Called the Grandfather's Dance, it is the customary way to end a festive evening in Nuremberg.

It is close to midnight when the last guests bid farewell. Sleepy but reluctant, Fritz and Clara are gently pulled off to bed.

As Clara is not allowed to take the Nutcracker to her room, she puts him in a doll's bed under the tree, drawing up the miniature woolen coverlets to his bandaged chin, against the cold, snowy night.

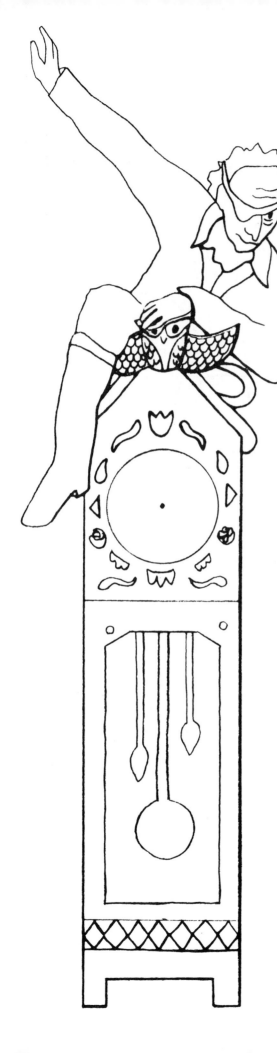

*U*nable to sleep, Clara creeps into the dark living room in her nightgown, carrying a candle. She checks to see how her Nutcracker is doing, tenderly removing him from the doll-bed. As Clara falls asleep on the couch, Drosselmeyer silently returns to repair the Nutcracker with his magic tools.

Clara awakens and tries to return her charge to his bed under the tree. But she is disturbed by unusual happenings.

The squeaking and scratching of scurrying mice across the floor seems to be growing as loud as human voices. The tall grandfather clock with the wooden owl on top is running at a frantic pace and in the irregular grinding of gears Clara hears,

"Clocks, clocks whir softly.

The King of the Mice
has a sharp ear.

Sing him his old song.

Sound his last hour --
for his fate is near."

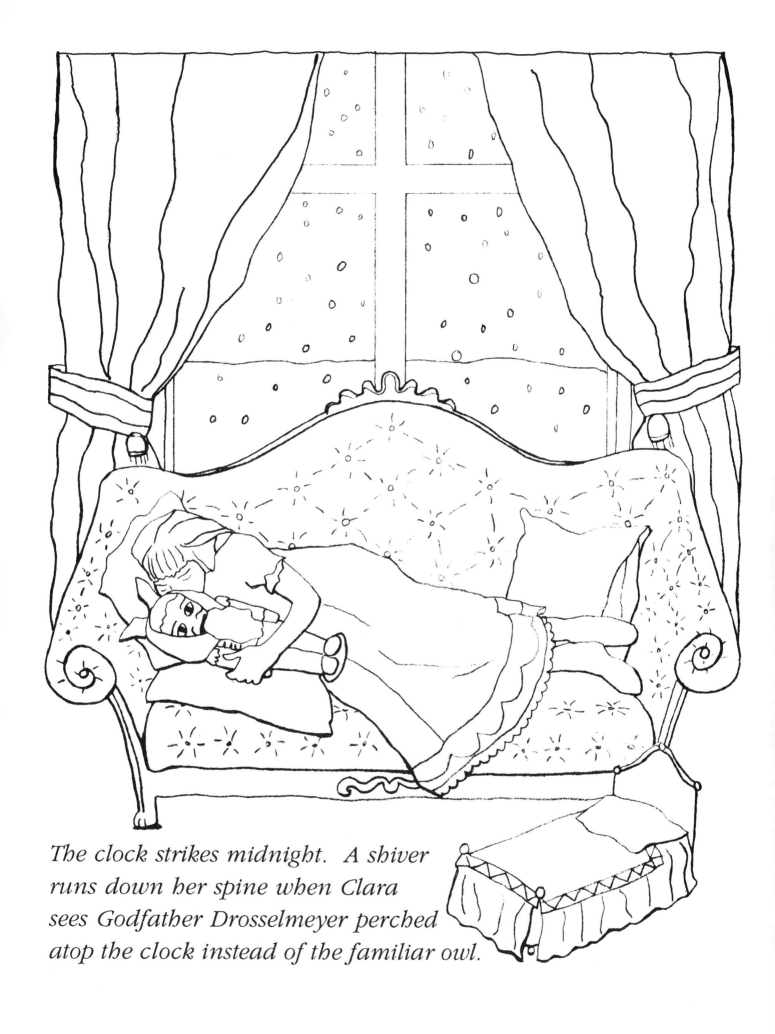

The clock strikes midnight. A shiver runs down her spine when Clara sees Godfather Drosselmeyer perched atop the clock instead of the familiar owl.

Hundreds of small lights appear to be shining from cracks in the wall until Clara begins to realize that these are really the eyes of giant mice that have grown to life-size. They look more like rats than mice, with their pointed noses and razor-sharp teeth gnawing ferociously on the pretty confections and presents still hanging on the tree. The rat-mice quickly organize themselves into the orderly ranks of a formidable army.

Most terrifying of all, suddenly a floorboard lifts and out pops their leader -- the King of the Mice -- with seven terrible heads, each wearing a golden crown, and each squeaking and shouting commands for the mouse army to obey.

Meanwhile the Christmas tree has grown as high as the ceiling, with ornaments and toys almost as big as Clara.

*T*he mouse army is confronted by a squadron of Fritz's finest toy soldiers, who have also grown to human size. They are led by a now full-sized Nutcracker.

The Nutcracker orders the toy cannon to be loaded with candy and fired at the invading mice. Although Fritz's soldiers fight valiantly, they are badly outnumbered.

With his troops forced to retreat, the Nutcracker tries to destroy the Mouse King in a sword duel. This too is going badly. Two of the mouse brigade have seized the poor Nutcracker by the cloak, holding him helpless so their commander can finish him off. All looks lost.

Then Clara, without thinking, takes off her slipper and throws it as hard as she can at the hideous Mouse King, who, *having pinned down the Nutcracker, is just about to run his sword through him.*

Clara's shoe hits its target squarely, knocking the enemy to the dusty floor. In seconds, the king and mice, armies and soldiers, all disappear magically into the dust.

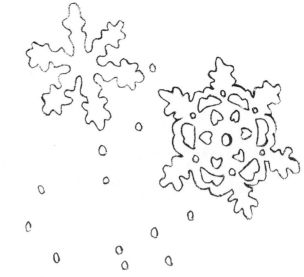

*A*t that very moment the Nutcracker is transformed into a handsome young Prince. He hands Clara the Mouse Kings' gold crowns, placing one of them on her head.

He is so grateful to her for saving his life that he invites her to the fantastic faraway Kingdom of Sweets. Clara gladly accepts, and the Prince, taking her by the hand, gallantly leads her away to his walnut boat which will speed them to their destination.

Their journey begins in the Land of Snow, as the living room becomes a forest. Clara's Christmas tree grows into the ground. The decorations hanging on it have melted into snow, which covers the branches in glistening whiteness.

The Prince navigates the small boat through the beautiful land which is covered with many trees like Clara's newly changed Christmas tree.

Deep in the forest of snow, the snowflakes gre

as the young couple are softly

them in a flurry of whirling, swirling motion,

...fted toward the Land of Sweets.

At last Clara and the Nutcracker Prince arrive at the castle of the lovely Sugar Plum Fairy, who rules over the Kingdom of Sweets. She and her courtiers welcome them warmly, placing a bouquet of freshly cut flowers in Clara's arms.

In her wildest dreams Clara could not imagine the splendor that now fills her widening eyes.

Everything is made of good things to eat. The palace walls and pillars are built out of hard candies of every color and flavor. The windows are decorated with sugar lace and pulled taffy shades. Even the marble floors are constructed of baked sugar almonds and raisins.

Gold and silver fruits hang from the trees. Shiny ribbons are blowing in the breeze, while a lemonade river rushes underfoot. They pass through a magnificent canopy of peppermint sticks and puffy meringue cookies.

*T*he Prince tells the story in pantomime of Clara's brave defeat of the Mouse King and his army of rat-mice. The Sugar Plum Fairy is most impressed.

With a wave of her magic wand she installs Clara and the Prince on a candy throne piled high with sugar lace, gingerbread men, ice cream cones, caramel custard, and peppermint canes. She sets a huge plate of chocolate bonbons before them.

To complete the celebration, the Sugar Plum Fairy arranges a command performance to entertain her special guests -- a succession of dances offered by the sweets and delicacies of the kingdom who have come to life in their honor.

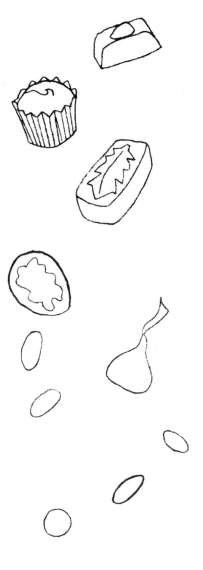

First an elegant pair of Spanish dancers portray the richest chocolate from Spain.

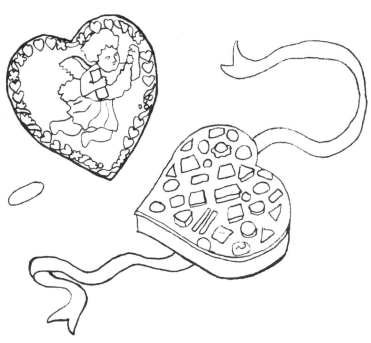

Exotic Arabian coffee is danced by a mysterious veiled beauty tinkling tiny finger symbols in her hands as she slinks smoothly through her steps.

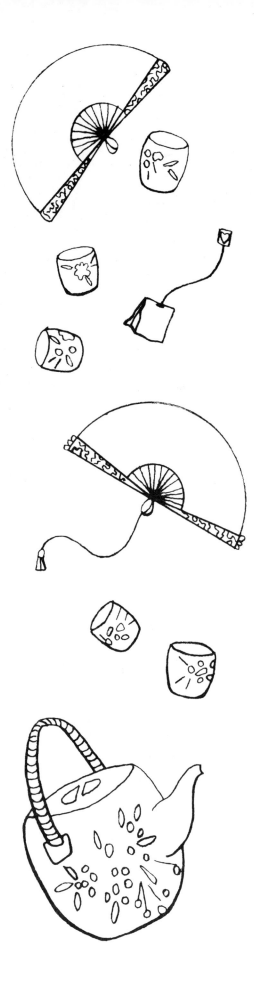

*T*angy
tea
from China
follows,
costumed in
colorful silk
brocades of
green jade
and orange
mango.

*T*he Candy Canes
appear, jumping lightly
through hoops that match
their red, white, and green
stripes, while Sugar Plum
looks on with approval.

Next
Marzipan
Shepherdesses
enter in a row,
piping sweet
melodies on their
reed flutes.

*M*other
Ginger
lifts her enormous
skirt and surprise!
Out scamper
her dancing
punchinella
children.

*T*hen the flowers from Clara's bouquet waltz exquisitely in a circle, fanning the air with their delicate perfume as they sweep across the floor in pastel hues: Violet, Rose, Hyacinth, Columbine, Dahlia, Carnation, Clematis, Rhododendron.

The last dance, performed by the Sugar Plum Fairy and her Cavalier, is the most beautiful of all. It is called the "grand pas de deux." Clara dreams that some day she will dance like that with her Prince.

*T*oo soon, the time has come to say goodbye, for it is Christmas morning. Clara and the Nutcracker Prince thank the Sugar Plum Fairy and, with the glittering Kingdom of Sweets still in view, they climb into a reindeer-drawn sleigh. The sleigh floats up like a balloon, then seems to drift backward toward a soft, female voice. "Clara, Clara," it calls, growing louder. "Time to get up."

Clara awakens in her bed, as the smell of freshly baked breakfast biscuits and a big hug from mother Stahlbaum welcome her back to the real-life adventures of a seven-year-old girl.

My Favorite *Nutcracker*

The story of <u>The Nutcracker</u> has been told so many different ways that it is nearly impossible to come up with a single, universal version. In some programs the young heroine, Clara, is played by a seven or eight year-old girl; in others she is danced by a grownup ballerina on pointe. Sometimes she is called Clara; other times she is Marie, and Clara is Marie's doll. Only the glorious Tchaikovsky music remains the same.

Place photo here.

Each of us remembers our favorite scenes in our own way. The fun is in the telling.

Autographs

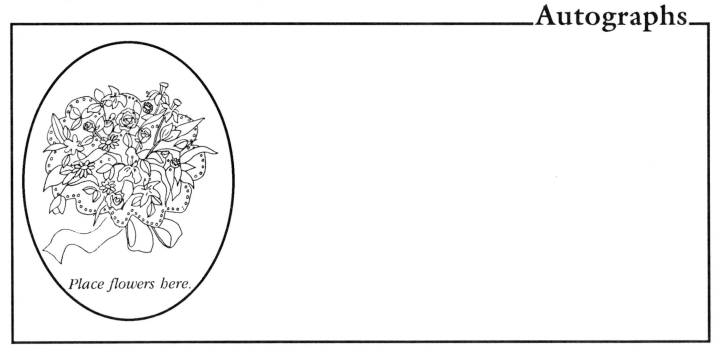

Place flowers here.